Kirlian Effect

Lori Lamothe

FUTURECYCLE PRESS
www.futurecycle.org

Cover artwork by Yuganov Konstantin; author photo by Lori Lamothe; cover and interior book design by Diane Kistner; Georgia text and Bradley Hand titling

Library of Congress Control Number: 2017950801

Published by FutureCycle Press
Athens, Georgia, USA

ISBN 978-1-942371-36-6

To those who sail in the wind's eye

Contents

1

And it says, "I burn."

—Robert Frost

Kirlian Effect

*Russian scientists discovered Kirlian photography during the 1940s.
It captures light that emanates from objects in electromagnetic fields.*

Phantom of a leaf
that's what they wrote in their notebooks.

No break in the light,
what was cut away minutes before

still part of the picture.
The leaf perfect, complete—

a ghost x-ray
held up against a square of night.

Look at energy's bones.
You can count them if you want to.

They're all there. Energy's bones
don't break, only shift

along the spectrum from health to sickness,
presence to absence.

They say the light shooting off the fingers and toes
of a newborn is blinding

but the man whose face
is falling backwards into his pillow

sleeps in a field of almost total darkness
as if God were standing in the room

dimming his soul. Death only a conduit,
the beating of the heart changed

into ordinary miracles—radios speaking,
phones ringing, coffeemakers clicking on.

If you pull the energy out straight,
you can see what a life

looks like after it unravels.
Then you can fasten loss around your neck

or let it drift like a white string
riding the wind of light-boned birds.

Red Mendelssohn

For two centuries sound disappeared—
the violin adrift in an attic or, worse,
unheard in a roomful of boarders smoking cigars.
Its color forgotten, its curves
locked in a coffin of silence.

There are stranger things than bad luck
so when music broke out again
in 1930s Berlin,
its woodfire notes crackling and disappearing in darkness,
we made the same damn mistake the Greeks
were always going on about.
Thought the barrier between men and gods
was a thing to be broken, easily,
with baroque abandon,
the way a child snaps a toy in two.

But the sparks flying from the place
where strings met bow were already suspect.
A few more years and the sheet music
Mendelssohn's great granddaughter played
would be shut up in silence.
Even the girl herself
would die in a car crash,
the melody of her life an echo in its shell.
The violin sold and eventually auctioned off,
bought by another grandfather
for another gifted girl.

Not a sad ending at all, really. Even so,
somewhere it's still too early for tragedy.
Somewhere Hitler still waits in the wings,
listening for his cue
as a sonata floats across a rented room
and waltzes with sunlight.

Baby

for Lilly

Born an addict
you flatlined
in a makeshift crib
detoxed at ten days
never knew your mother
may someday recall
vaguely a father
who showed up
on occasion
reeking anger
but this morning
your forever is
now is whatever
both hands grasp
as you touch
the world alive
alive alive in spring
light, honeyed air.

Dinosaur Tracks

after Edward Hitchcock (1793-1864)

You found them before the word or even the idea
existed. The three-toed prints scattered across sandstone
muddying an image of perfection, a creation
minus mistakes. Some said they were the marks
of Noah's raven, a letter its dark wings
wrote to the land or maybe even God himself—
the etchings a reproach to the rainbow
peaking out from behind clouds, its pretty apology
floating just out of reach. Others less fanciful
believed the impressions were made by turkeys and left it
at that. The material world a straightforward place
filled with hard-working people, loyal animals,
simple birds uninterested in flight. You didn't know
what to think but grasped at fossils of enormous,
ancient feathers, long legs and necks, wide beaks
that would explain this piece of His unsolved puzzle.
Still, at night in dreams you hunted for a form
to hold the pictures that ruled your jungle of imagination—
waited for language to claim that huge, flickering
moment between existence and extinction.

Girls Jumping on Trampolines

They flicker in and out
of focus—summer caught

between them as their hair
flames out across blue.

The day's been drawn out
to a single long syllable,

but of course one jumps higher,
burns recklessly brighter

as she floats in expectation.
And I can't help wondering

which of the two will master
our ordinary hells—

the wise-eyed sister
who stitches caution

onto regulation socks
or the one with feathers

tucked between thin shoulders—
everything we thought

we knew dissolving
as she rises

into sky's unanswered
question.

Jellyfish

We stop counting at ten,
the beach a bloom of transparency—

as if the storm had pressed
its fingerprints onto sand.

Strange though, this clarity
that hides inside itself.

Dead or alive—we can't tell
the difference, can only guess

at images of what must have been
beautiful. We tell ourselves

it's too late for small-scale heroics—
leave them shining across noon

like broken glass. Hours later
there's nothing left—their bodies

reborn as clouds crossing water,
as rain falling through light

onto a field of open umbrellas—
the sea a dark flowering

drifting endless toward shore.

Ohio

The summer we drove over the border
into Kentucky, I waited for the grass
to turn suddenly blue,
as if there were places in the world
where you could cross into extraordinary.
It was the month of fireflies,
the month when the sun set late
and our apartment building
rose higher than any home I'd known.
In the car after dark, I pretended to speak
a different language, exotic and untranslatable,
babbling jabberwocky words
until my parents hushed me.
Even then I wanted untouchable things.
Happiness tethered to the moon's cloud mane
as my mind raced toward magic,
ignoring life's bit and gripping any illusion
that would take me
all the way toward impossible.

Bottle Tree, 1922

At night it sings
every branch

heavy with badness.
I lie in bed

listening to the
caught spirits

storming inside
blue glass

touch my hand to
my throat

feel the want
beating humming-

bird wings
quick like love

for the wrong
man the heart

thrashing in its cage
mad for freedom.

Moonshine.
Moonshine.

The whiskey dark
against my skin.

I close my eyes
pray for dawn

to burn off desire
stain the world pink.

Glass Town

A shattered windshield woke us
out of no sleep, a night of trees
snapped in two. The woods
echoing with the sound of gunshots
or maybe just God popping some
supernatural version of bubble wrap.
The world as we didn't know it
encased in ice, everything shining,
blinding, melting before us.
Power lines glittered low
or hissed warnings in tongues.
An entire neighborhood turned from wood
to crystal, its children imprisoned
in the storm's snow globe gleam.

You weren't sure what to think,
eight being an age of wonder still.
Even the pine fallen across the roof
seemed dangerous in a way you couldn't
resist. But there was fear, too.
Caught up in silence, you watched the sky
erase its work over and over,
saw how darkness spilt all the way to horizon,
blacker than anything you understood.

As for me, I wasn't sure either.
The cold slithered over our coats,
sank its fangs into the furniture.
I studied the branches of your small bones
and conjured your skeleton scattered across death's
frozen pond. I heard the jangled music
of the house falling in on itself
and covered my ears against imagining.
But that wasn't all of it. Huddled
inside our circle of wavering light,
I felt the part of me I'd laid away
like an old nightgown at the bottom of a drawer
float out of hiding and reach across safety
to touch its sleeves to flame.

Scary Movie

There's always an old house,
clapboard or stone—
it doesn't really matter which
as long as it appears at the end of a path
that winds all the way
to the heart of fear's labyrinth.
If there's a dollhouse, even better.
Let its owner peer through the windows
and see herself in miniature,
her life reclining safe
on the surface of childhood.
Let her not remember yet
how night's bony finger
used to tap out a summons
from inside its coffin.

Instead, instruct her to open
the tiny music box
no bigger than a fingertip.
Note the way its tune
haunts her sanity
in predictable increments
until there's nothing left of her mind
but the ghosts whose voices
ring out across reason.
But know, too, that in this
version of suffering she will always
find the staircase curving away from terror—
that before the credits roll,
she'll unlock the past's rusted door
and stumble back into happiness.

Rothko No. 8, 1952

Silence is so accurate. —Mark Rothko

At first, the intensity seems
easy as simple math—
language minus its meanings,
shadow subtracted from brightness.

It's the kind of formula
that leaves even the suicides
tap dancing like madmen
on the heads of ghostly pins.

Atoms of radiance, splitting
into a million mirrored suns and that's all—
happiness painted so large
there isn't any room for metaphor,

or tints of dusk, or clouds of doubt
casting spells of veils and rain.
It's not until you reach the end of looking
that you realize you're on the wrong side of euphoria,

that the painting is actually a window—
a window somebody came along
and slammed shut
before you ever arrived.

Or maybe once, a long time ago,
on a day you don't remember, you rambled in the forever
of that childhood, oblivious to the echoes
of your name rippling across the distance to night.

All Hallow's Eve

The line straggles past severed
hands and bloody feet
lopped off at the ankles.
We're surrounded by skeletons,
bags of eyeballs, pale babies
with bland, unblinking gazes,
our progress marked
by the sound of a scream
repeating itself all the way
to hell. Back home, you ring
your eyes with gloom,
apply scars in obvious places.
For tonight, all our fears
are nothing but a hood slipped
onto life—darkness a dream
spliced with fake blood
and old horror flicks.
On a tray in the kitchen
a dozen apples gleam black
in sweet, hard shells—
as if the taste of death
were only a temptation
too sweet to resist.

North Leominster, 1967

Who's that behind those Foster Grants?

A boy dyed green
emerges out of the river.
His friend laughs,
ignores the trees—
how they cast shadows
across the afternoon.
Nothing will happen,
he thinks to himself,
the sheen of alien skin
only a costume—
the kind of change
that flows down a drain,
forgotten before bed.
His dreams are full
of girls in sunglasses.
In miniskirts and platform
shoes, they lean back
against leather interiors,
their blonde hair
flying out behind them
like an ad for freedom.
Years later, his daughter
rocks herself to sleep,
her world locked inside
itself, her perception
a country of one.
At night he stands
just outside its borders,
his hand held above
her crib, wishing
he could reach down
and touch her small form,
open a door into all
the dreams he can't see.

August

Night hovers at the edge of the porch.

Heat's blue swelter
is finally on its way out,
and a song drifts through an open window.

The lyrics flicker against the light I've left on for you,
translucent words
without any understanding of fear.

I sit in a wicker chair as they disappear into darkness
like ghosts of summers I can't call back.

Conservatory

*The imago is the last stage an insect attains during
its metamorphosis, its process of growth and development;
it also is called the imaginal stage.*

          Wings opening across azure,
my sweater a sky   momentary
substitute for flight   and all at once
I'm a field of air   sleeves flickering
colors   winged flowers.
At once I'm my own sun   burning
motion   casting off
beauty's weird little flares.

The woman beside me disagrees.
They think you're water   she says,
iPhone aimed at her son
                    waiting statue still
for transformation   or maybe
only the swallowtail end of patience.

When we leave, an attendant checks
for stray species,
                scans our backs,
our streaming hair   our solid ground shoes,
but we're blank as absence,
our bodies their names unspoken.

Outside, passersby walk concrete paths,
heavy in their bones,
but there are wings inside my cupped hands
      closing and unclosing,
imago   breathing me again blue
as water, as air.

Still Life with Lawn Display

Baby Jesus sings "Greensleeves"
as a herd of phosphorescent reindeer
weighs down the roof.
It's as though the season's stuck
on repeat—the same brittle snowmen
forever blinking S.O.S signals
back and forth in tacky unity.
Even Homer Simpson's ready to call it quits—
begs a pair of texting siblings to stab his blown-up
belly with no. 2 pencils.

Who among us hasn't made the leap
from A to B—concocted
a manifesto on our inclination
to Honey Boo Boo sacred things
into a dialect of Kardashian?
Snapchat, tweet, post everything
in America that's gone missing
on a milk carton no one will ever read.
Whisper an incantation of dire proportions
or pray an unbranded God
will send down a plague of identity theft—
blacken our shiny extravagance
with fierce, unforgiving lightning.

Along a lit fence, a kid alone inside his abuse
laughs at night's madcap carnival cruise,
then erases sound
before anyone else can hear him.
And maybe I take it all back.
Or maybe I don't.

Children Imitating Airplanes

You read the subtitle and smile
at the line of children tilting their arms
this way and that,
their bodies a ragged chain snaking across a city square,
their minds flying unfriendly skies
that would never harm them.

Innocence is like that. Or at least
it should be. You don't know
about the kids in the movie that will end in tears
or the ones long gone, the actual kids
who played at war until sky opened its mouth
and swallowed them whole.
What they knew of happiness.

Sometimes you crave it for yourself—
you can't help it. The blue heights.
Wings. Sunlight bouncing off clarity—
the quilted land sprawled out before you
like a warm, made-up place.

The shining world. How badly you want it
sometimes. On the commute home
you press your foot to the accelerator,
feel the engine hum fantasy
as the impossible fuselage of years
gains speed and a sudden shock of air
lifts you out of yourself.

Birch Forest, 1903

after Gustav Klimt

There's something antique about them—
the way they cluster together at the edge of the field,
willowy, white trunks
standing not quite straight
like tall girls at a high school dance.

Of course they're beautiful, dressed
as they are in September. All day
they rustle the sort of answers teachers want to hear—
a short, sweet music of compliance.
All day they bend under the wind's instruction,
their yellow leaves lifting and turning
until they dissolve into sky—
frailty a series of notes on a recorder,
a tune anyone could play.

It's only at night, when the moon
comes to wash the landscape in absence,
that they step out of ordinary.
Stripped of the sun's too-strong light,
they gleam in darkness, the world
a dance of secrets, a dreaming of fugues,
a luminous calculus of possibilities.

Coming Attractions

Morning opens its door on scoured light
and sweeps my cluttered rooms.

The sky's been rinsed with wind,
the land bleached down to its bone.

October was a lit match—every shade
of tree on fire, the lawn a sheet

strewn with leaves redder than petals.
There are women who shouldn't

wear mascara. There are poems of glass,
all windows, that you can open

to observe a ghost's beating heart.
Note how each chamber

serves as its own paperweight—
how a wing's blue pulse

is actually a lake that mirrors lightning.
The switch of our attention

flickers as the day scrolls down
to a hotel for professional snugglers

that might be a treasure map,
might be a brothel.

Cross Country

We're on a road trip to nowhere,
where your ex-half brother
will belt out his heart on a stage
while the light never hits its mark.
Behind us: Graceland with its red felt
pool table and Twinkie offerings,
arguments, no sex, some talk about aliens,
and a couple in new Orleans
who bought us Hurricanes in exchange
for what we wouldn't do. It's been years
since we spoke. I don't remember
your voice or your middle name,
only the moment when the Texas sky
filled with lightning and you held my hand
because neither of us knew if the wide
rain-soaked future held inside it
emptiness or freedom.

Interior

Now winter is a blue bowl, red blocks,
light that shines familiar shapes.
                              If it snows
we can watch the fire weaving its colors
or climb a ladder of numbers
until we reach the tips of the universe
where planets sit round the stars and tell stories.

Now life has settled over us, and the past
is only a pond that's frozen
in the base of a spoon.
                      If I want to,
I can skate across its surface
and come to the other side of regret.

Van Gogh

At the museum
Jesus' sweet head
sags to one side
and a dead king's dogs
hunt boar beyond the glare.

One room over   the light
                  melts

as a stolid row of rooftops
previously fading
in pale-sun sanity

          flames into a polka.

Reading

at the Peabody-Essex Museum

On the other side of glass
a band plays marching songs
and the leaves
flicker green fire.
The poet tries to ignore what everybody else
isn't, tries to fasten our attention to the words,
drapes cadence
over the chandelier,
the podium, the folding chairs.
But it's spring and the world shines like a new puzzle—
each window pane a promise
that this is the year
we're going to solve everything.

2

Did He who made the lamb make thee?
—William Blake

Dragon

Some days the fire in me
flickers at the border of out.
It's a country I don't
want to visit, living here
as I do, my mind a cave
of scattered light, muffled
weather. Off in a corner
my mother's bones gleam,
wrapped in shadows.
I don't know where it sleeps,
this thing inside me
that heaps rage onto a pyre
and makes destruction blaze,
burns kingdoms whole.
Don't know why when it's over
I slink back to safety—sated,
belly bloated with rubies,
keychains and copper bowls
tucked under my wings.
At night I polish silverplate
until the useless shines—
see myself in spoons,
turned small and upside down.

Bottle Tree, 1831

He treated her with personal violence.
—from a petition to pardon Frankie Silver,
who killed her husband with an axe

They say it's sunlight
that kills them—

spirits caged
inside blue glass,

the evil in them
dazzled by beauty,

burned beyond seeing.
Early morning.

Sheets flapping
on the line,

the baby asleep
in her crib, breath

wrapped snug
in a dream,

the day soft,
soft. Last night's

storm—bruise of
clouds, split-lip sky—

gone, gone,
all the violence

siphoned into eternity
like water

funneling
down a drain.

On the other side
of a screen door,

wind traces its fingertips
over gaps in

silence, sings
lullabies to God.

Skeletons

One lies curled up in emptiness
without even a name for a blanket.

Another scatters across a whispering sand,
a wind of shapeless sounds.

The bones know nothing of beauty.
They gleam in the noontime sun.

At dusk the blood-red sky runs its fingertips
over a curve of pelvis, an ulna's

delicate tapering, and darkness comes
to grope strands of highway, blue ribbons

unraveling all the way to oblivion
under a cold, star-spangled heaven.

Ghost Hunters

at the Rutland Prison Camp Ruins

We ask questions of grass,
darkness, an owl's screech.
As for the dead, they don't
comment, forward all inquiries
to the stones that aren't
there. Graves unmarked,
lives nameless, crimes
forgotten or erased
off the spirit maps
we've shoved into back pockets
of skepticism. Someone
wants to know if they're at last
at peace, if they've found
redemption or remorse,
if the stopped voices
floated up from dried flowers
and coaxed them at last
toward understanding or maybe
just memory, just that.

The bones have nothing to tell us.
Our recorders go on fingerprinting silence,
its whorls and loops
to be analyzed at a later time.
In the clearing, the moon bleaches absence.

Polaroid with Extra Processing

You say the party is *a shade of blue you don't care for* even though
it's a red-eye flight through house music, its thunder-thigh vibrations.
You hope he mentions Zelda, that flapper mind, that white-heat madness.
You're that drunk, that naïve. Instead he says you look like Jodie Foster,
but you know he really means Clarice with her rube shoes and cheap bag.
Outside, in the clear air under a star-spangled sky, Megen with an *e*,
about to travel the world someday, tells you writers *do the work* and
asks about the scar on your neck. You tell the same old cigarette burn
lie as she turns toward an Irish waitress whose hair flames Dante.
The scent of rain mists you toward sleep as you imagine disappearing
inside the darkness. You count poets and romance novel heroes,
men you've slept with and men you haven't, the names of cities, roses,
cousins you haven't seen in years. The words bloom on your tongue:
Dickinson Neruda Rilke. Duncan John Raif. Nairobi Nashville Berlin.
Orange Dream Lemon Drop Blue Moon. Missy Melanie Stacey.
The syllables petals of sound curling, unfurling, fading. Meanings
scattering across black inattentive sky.

The Cardiff Giant

*Word of his presence quickly spread, and soon thousands
of people were making the journey out to Stub Newell's farm
to see the colossus. —Museum of Hoaxes*

We kept going back. Even after the archaeologist
pointed out chisel marks across the face,
explained in simple terms the ease
with which knitting needles can replicate
supernatural pores. Of course we doubted.
Maybe knew. But it was an idea we couldn't
let go of: that half-heaven of fallen angels
taking seven-league strides from field to
field. Smashing Everests, dousing volcanoes,
dragging chastity down to hell. At night
we dreamt enormous wings hidden under
ordinary muscle, bulky coats. What did we care
if a paleontologist from Yale called it humbug?
There were giants in the earth in those days.
Back home, loaves burned in the oven, children
cried, washing accumulated. Our husbands
paid the priest in town to tell us he wasn't
an angel at all, only an out-of-work carnival freak
who split a geode, drank its contents, and turned
to stone. We kept going back.

The Agoraphobic's Dream

A few moments scatter across the beach.
They flame up from our footprints
like trick birthday candles or dusk's
resurrected dogs. Foaming shore,
solid-sky distance, closeness of your voice,
of wind waving grass, umbrellas tilting.

Here light bounces off everything tangible—
shells and broken glass, sand and horizon,
screech of gulls, the sea. If I close my eyes,
the glare diamonding water is still
blinding. Fire haunts my skin, my hair,
settles onto words I've collected
in my bucket of silence. Reality's
sticky, a grit between my teeth,
the kind of glitter that won't wash off.

I don't know if I'm a coward or not.
I don't know what you'd say if I asked
because I don't ask. Either way
I'm fluent in the language of fear,
can shutter my mind against angles
in a single bound, wrap moth wings in wool
for safekeeping. Don't get me wrong.
Tomorrow I'll walk tightropes with strings of hearts
tied round my ankles, write your name in circles
across the blue, blue air.

To the Guy Who Posted about Kittens on His Doorstep

Take care of the kittens jerk ass.
—Craigslist reader

You can forget about the girl.
Nobody admits to adding more tape
to a box of cuteness
and expects karma to issue a pardon.

You're on your own now. Better
to make use of your box cutter
and watch them scatter
across Darwin's concrete.

Why not? At first the lightness
of the box will astound you,
and for once the silence won't
remind you you're single.

But it's never that easy, setting
mistakes free. At night, in dreams,
they always find their way back—
tales flickering orange fire,

little eyes aglow, little sandpaper
tongues licking at guilt
like candles that won't blow out
or riddles you can't solve.

Mind Fishing

The front yard's a galaxy of yellow—
every last petal burning steady

like candles that won't
blow out.

I'm skeptical about color like that.

Some days I'm a girl so long untethered
the only light that reaches me

is a desert of dead stars.

Some days tangerines and hawks,
a lace collar, certain words,

a chipped door painted blue

reel me closer even as I'm slipping
off the hook cast into existence.

And I still don't know why
it scares me—

the gravity of ordinary things.

Let At Least the Sky, the Rain

The peonies in the yard
hold their fists tightly closed,
ready for a fight,

as a lone ant roams from globe
to globe in search of an unlocked door,
a window into softness.

It's dusk. Late Spring. My twitter feed
is full of adsong and the real birds
in the real trees have gone silent.

Friends are all vacationing in exotic locales,
apparently. There's nothing on TV.

Meanwhile darkness gathers at the edge
of light, waits behind the curtains of the pines
for its cue,

and for no reason I remember
driving by an enormous red barn,
its doors loftily closed.

Almost losing a tire. The wild grind
before the swerve.

Cities. Baseball. Rival pitchers
battling it out. A story
about a rare albino raven
murdered

and a chaos of roses sparking last summer
as they spilled over a fence.

I don't know what any of it means
or if it means anything at all.
I don't know what I'm waiting for
or even if I'm waiting.

Tonight let me dream lightning.
Let at least the rain open itself to me

and touch (with its mild, invisible fingertips) my face
(at least, at least).

Still Life

There's a newspaper open across the table,
a cat called cat
perched like a bird on the rim of a chair,
and her blue-black hair
is washed in ordinary shadows.

It was one of those decades
when people read things cover to cover
in a single sitting; when snowflakes
drifted across makeshift goals;
when summer's blue burning
hibernated behind houses.

By her side, an untuned piano
stands immovable at the center of silence,
the world inside and out
just as weighted. At least that's how
I imagine it—grainy winter light
battened down and everything close
lulled by the far-flung whistle
of a train rumbling toward night.

Ritual

after Anna Akhmatova

Hands, matches, ashtray.
The curling of paper always
the same. Flames licking
wisps of clouds, of moon;
the ring of silver spurs,
a crust of snow,
a constellation of stones
cast into a well's deep coolness.
Inside the walls the bugs
stop to listen,
snap their jaws,
then grow bored with
the smoking images,
the ash of words
unspoken, unread.
Somewhere a guard
flings a gray blanket
onto your son's sleepless
form. Somewhere else,
inside an ordinary afternoon,
a poet sips tea
before reciting Eliot, Frost,
Tennyson. And somewhere
close—so close you can
lean out your window
and inhale its ice into your lungs—
the terrible ghost
that pretends to be your city
flickers on, flickers off.
as night spreads its cape over sound.
Hands, matches, ashtray.

At the Kitchen Window

November. My mind's full of dark interiors,
corridors of words
                tunneling toward the heart.

Its chambers echo the way new houses do.
I want to fill them with the kind of furniture
that presses clawed feet into
                hard floors,
carves grooves in memory.

Outside, twin metal poles tilt away from each other
at awkward angles, the lines that bound them
    long gone.

The bird feeder has slipped into silence.

The garden's a scribble of neglect.

Even the season has burned to the quick.
    Its orange leaves
gutter in evening's lamp

but the future's been there all along, waiting
with its crimson feathers,
    its Etch-A-Sketch birdsong,
its Foxglove bells that ring out across the stillness
    and shock vision back into beating.

Wintering

To wrap ourselves in red   suddenly
seems essential   not as heat
as fire engine sirens   five-alarm
fucking   the kind that slams loneliness
up against   walls
rips off   its panties.

I don't want seduction   slinking around
inside my mind   draping appeal over an idea
of a drop-dead body   wearing only a bow—
anticipation   a present
waiting   to be opened.

In summer   it didn't matter
or anyway I didn't   notice the space
where roses would be   the gap
between sunup   and sundown
harmless   as a kid's crooked smile.

But now I need   to fill drawers
with vermilion sweaters   set wool socks
ablaze   feel the old burn
of whiskey
                    on its way
                              down.

Moscow

Across the street from the bus stop
a black dog lay dead for weeks.
Every day the temperature bit my hands,
knocked my mind out cold.
Every day thin, gray flakes swirled out of sky
and I felt myself falling too, tumbling headlong
into the kind of numbness
people don't always wake up from.

That winter the waiters didn't smile for no tips
and the language caught on my tongue.
Somebody needs to do something,
I tried to tell my tutor, a man I slept with,
an ambulance driver who traded rides for Marlboros.
Nobody listened, or maybe it was meaning
that wouldn't comply—
my lake of words finally frozen
all the way through.

I wanted to name him. On the way back
from techno clubs, I hummed "The Star-Spangled Banner"
for no reason in particular and watched
the clouds of my breath float into existence,
only to dissolve in night.
The names were like that, too.
Lucky. Buddy. Sasha. Pavlov.
The syllables rose and set at regular intervals,
burning bright holes in emptiness.
One day he was gone and I wished him
back into presence with no success,
selfish in my longing
for one dark, familiar thing.

Migratory

It's true—that the two sisters
in their car buried deep in wind and shifting snow
survived (for weeks)
on melted ice and Girl Scout cookies.

I'm not going to lie.
I sometimes exist vicariously via this kind of thing—
(for weeks)
fill the emptiness inside
with shot after sweet dopey shot
of the sensational.

This morning I took my infatuation in my fist,
smashed it around the insides of this poem
until the bars of the lines
bent to make a cage
for your winged heart.

What does it matter? Somewhere it flutters
crimson in the cage of your body
regardless—
thrashing against life until it almost (every
time) cracks dawn in two
and flies (where?)—

Morning After

We woke to the shock of weather
too beautiful to last. Yesterday's
ordinary world encased in ice,
the yard an unshaken snow globe—
all the branches of landscape
set in stopped time. No wind, no motion,
not even the dripping of water
onto accumulated things.

Part of me wants it to go on,
this stillness inside and out—this
morning held in stasis like a clock in a net
or a heart past beating. But only a part
of me. Change has its own striptease,
its own brand of seduction—
a lingerie of self-destruction
written in red skies rising
across pale, sleepy lawns.

Nocturne #2

at Race Point Beach

Atop a rise in the distance, a square
of light against blue-black sky.

To my right, a fox not full-grown,
far-wandered from its family.

Baby fox, yellow window,
and the usual tumult
tucked safe inside my chest.

Can you triangulate loneliness?

Shape three singularities into one
the way a clock goes on chasing its tail
until the seconds blur to infinite?

The fox ambled off without offering any
information.

The yellow light bloomed in darkness,
its warmth a kind of protest
against our broken trinity.

As for me, I turned back toward the place
I started from,
all elbows and irreconcilable angles—

life its own galaxy
so many stars from home.

Black Sheep Café

The woman across the room is signing copies
of instability's cookbook, her pen name

a nervous breakdown of broken chords.
You push your chair out of earshot

from a murder of crows dressed in matching
feathers, foiling their random forays

into intimacy as if *distance* is your superhero
power. Still, it's hard not to notice

how night yawns bottomless from your cup,
how you've swirled lesser transgressions

into darkness for good measure—the Thanksgiving
you leapt out of protocol and wrapped both hands

around your sister's spidery version of *nice,*
the Easter you set your hair on fire

and tap-danced his unspoken name
across a polished table. Or maybe not.

Maybe all you ever did was touch knife to fork,
lay your napkin in your lap, and pass the condiments

clockwise. Either way, the past blurs beyond
recording, the keys to reality whirring

player piano songs, the music of seconds
unraveling too fast for transcription.

On the far side of the fish bowl,
bolts of sky billow waves of blue,

rolling out oceans of color any of us
could sail from here to beauty's horizon.

Little Risks

*The glass delusion is an extraordinary psychiatric phenomenon
in which people believe themselves to be made of glass.*
—Victoria Shepherd

A man whose mind may break
requests asylum
in a padded room.
He fears the ire of chairs
and table edges,
floors so slick with wax
they shine puddles and shattered mirrors.
He fears the women in white
who float unseen around corners,
all elbows and invisible angles.

At night his dreams pace corridors.
His body still, still,
his breath a wind battened down,
his bones shuttered and the world
turned interior.

This morning I stepped out the front
door, slid a key into the ignition,
and waited for routine
to scatter the usual sparks across gasoline—
every day a letter read so many times
life's worn down to translucence.
In parking lots daylight falls
and goes on falling through me,
burns holes in my shadow.

Sanibel Island

In the 1920s poet-psychiatrist Merrill Moore, author of more than 50,000 sonnets, transported boxes of seashells north for his patients to sort as part of their therapy.

At first it was the sea you wanted. And sky—
all that space, that blue. The simple blinding sun

  enveloping everything in its warmth
  without ever getting too close,

the figures that cast shadows across the beach
for once in proper perspective. Words

like *anguish,* like *mutilation,* like *involuntary
pathology fragmentation prescription institution*

  almost undetectable, their syllables
  bleached hollow by the waves

crashing along the shore. But it would be too
much—to let infinity with its God-sized breakers

pound against the mind's marooned glass.
The only possible outcome a trickle of sunset

snaking its way down a wrist, a sleep
that reaches all the way to horizon.

          What else, then?

You dug them up yourself, the shells. Scooped
them out of sand by the hundreds, the thousands,

and shipped the whole cargo north, where white-
capped nurses in red brick buildings would overturn

order and spill its contents across empty tables.
You still weren't sure, though, if it would work

for them, too—the elixir of sorting beauty into form.

Forecast

At the border between properties,
a galvanized washtub collects falling
snow. Hours later, the white's risen
so high it brims over emptiness.
I want to kneel down before it
and rinse my bare arms in its cold,
clean comfort. I want to let the idea of
an original, untouched world accumulate
because there are so many spaces inside me
waiting for renewal. The heart with its huge
barn doors thrown open in anticipation
of love's galloping horses. The mind
and its attic of memories. Even the hands
held out for work, for its solid, familiar tools.
Above me, the clouds open their trap doors
all at once and flakes sift down, blanketing
everything with a marvelous innocence
that will surely last long enough this time.

3

...his raptures were all air and fire.
—Michael Drayton

The Blue Earrings

For months I've kept the universe
in a box. It happens.

I get tired of infinity
with its sapphire eyes

staring out at me
from behind mirrors.

But today when I slip on
all that sea, that sky,

everything immense
seems a little

lighter, as if nature
isn't so in-your-face

endless after all—
or maybe I've just gotten

used to the idea of
this big flickering life

being so damned brief.

Painting with Scissors

after Henri Matisse

Parakeets and mermaids,
clowns and jazz, nudes
and a scattering of yellow
star-suns bursting. Life
exploding into being
as a blue window opens
beside a blue window—
the walls of your bedroom
reeling with color, paper,
forms freed from predictable
patterns.

On the other side of art, Hitler
brings his fist down onto a map.
You stay where you are,
wheel your old, broken body
in and out of danger one more day.
The scissors in your hand flash
an unvanquished joy
as the confetti universe
scatters itself at your feet.

The Snow Is Always Greener

Last winter snow fell to the rooftops,
piled in drifts against doors and windows.
Bicyclists pedaled through tunnels of ice
as the house weathered
storm after storm, its yellow lamps
invisible behind frosted glass.
We hunkered down inside ourselves,
dreaming green canticles, apple blossoms.
Spring, we thought (no, we *knew*)
was all that mattered.

Today flakes swirl out of a mild-mannered sky
and wipe their prints off every surface.
They leave no trace of the wind's
ever-changing whimsy,
what the clouds thundered.
In the yard, fog envelopes everything
in its cool, mystical embrace,
lulls the pines to sleep as if life
were a delicate, ghostly thing.

We've never been sure what we wanted,
but sometimes it's hard not to think
of how the cold raged and the night
whirled around us. How we grew together
to form a center no world could shake.
And when we remember the candled glow
of oranges in a bowl at the center of the table,
we can't help wondering
why we didn't want it to last.

The House

is not a shell, echoes ping-
ponging off every wall,
knocking lamps helter
skelter and shattering
orphaned wine glasses.
More like one of those
Russian dolls nobody
knows the name for
but is always using as
a metaphor for the word
secrets, the word *depth,*
the idea of *an onion*
unfolding ugly petals
in an impression of crying.
Open it, the house
and all its little painted faces.
Line them up across the years
in descending order.
Or, if you'd rather, stand
with your mind's knife
before the cutting board
of the past and peel away
layers of wood, of stone
until you reach love's
coppery sheen or a life
blinking out. Remember
a man who sat transparent
on the edge of the bed
and spoke about threshing
sky for gold. See your
daughter streaming
in and out of selves,
childhood blurring by
like the flip book she
made for you in first grade.
At last recall the fingerprint
of the voice of the old
owner who told stories
about her six dogs rambling

in wild, unmown lawn
when you know for a fact
there were no dogs, no ramblings, no
unmown lawns—only a black
cat and a carved
high chair for no infant
ornate in its silence.

The Explorer's Dream

In 1820, Arctic explorer William Scoresby arranged these shapes into a formal classification scheme, which included, in addition to the six-pointed stars, such forms as needle-like hexagonal prismatic columns... —Philip Ball

After so much winter
it was impossible not to think of snow
as a blank page—
the mind numb to everything endless,
the world an unwritten letter,
a silence unbroken.
My wife at home before fires burning,
our sons vanquishing imaginary.
What was there to say?
This eternity a monster without name.

After enough time anybody
can fall into a tunnel of zeros,
slide down absence and emerge in a landscape
where logic blooms upside down.
It wasn't until it happened I understood
there are seas where depths are warmer than surfaces,
that a single sheet of white
can shine fields of infinities.

The Orchid Keeper's Dream

I've always wanted to be the one
who fills in the blanks. At night I conjure

lips pressed to the usual hollows,
the spaces beating hummingbird wings,

hear my voice breathe warmth into
the room where we began, where we

would begin—hands signing instructions
for touch in seven lost languages.

Maybe you think I'm talking about
emptiness, about regret. I'm not.

Greenhouse heat fills the days,
life dappled with bloom. At dusk

the sun slants through glass
and the slender curves of stems

bend toward grace. Note how
each petal holds the light inside it.

Note that the petals don't exist.
You can't imagine their delicacy,

the dazzling, invisible air.

Tracks

at the Beneski Museum of Natural History

There's something delicate about them,
these three-toed impressions

scattered across gray slabs
like a dead poet's cursive

slanting toward transformation.
The room's full of them,

spidery, shifting journeys
that begin and end in silence,

unanswered questions. We'll never
know if the words opened their doors

for the poet or what they had to say
about eternity, if anything.

As for the tracks, their message
can't be translated either.

Maybe they're notes minus
sound, each print

a score of stars, a darker shadow
of a god burning to write

the symphony of everything,
over and over, until the music

of imagination ripples out
across time's bottomless lake.

Or maybe there is no God,
no pattern, not even

one accidental, elegant riff
waiting for science

to transcribe its measure
onto a new theory.

Outside, every leaf
hums quantum music.

Listen, the sun's playing
its red violin.

X-Ray

Small bones,
the technician
tells me, coaxing
a curve of spine
into place, like
photographing
a blade of grass.
I wonder where
she is, this ghost
of a girl—all frailty
and spirit—locked
inside my body's
cage. I want
to pin her picture
up against light,
study the map
of her skeleton
and chart a path
to the heart
of strangeness.
When I get there
I'll lay my palms
across her back
and reach until I
feel the filaments
of wings, the unseen
architecture of song,
thrashing under my
grip—mad to break
the hold of such
ordinary hands.

Linnaeus

Runners cut across the world's blank page,
the snow beneath the sledge blindingly white.

Seventy years of learning and every name
erased, the years and the faces blurred

beyond recognition. All morning you
grasped at old words with both hands,

unwilling to let go. Once a long time ago
you went out in summer light to laugh

at the wild birds parroting nomenclatures,
the monkeys making a mess of God's garden.

Nights you stole lanterns and crept into darkness
to study the sleep of plants. The idea was to make

sense of all things—the exotic, the overlooked,
the mysterious. What if the answer to the riddle

of existence was a seed so tiny it lay dreaming
in some far-flung latitude? Now it's too late

for solving. Better to lose yourself in an incandescence
of afternoon. Wisps of clouds brightening vague

vanilla sky. The wind through the trees singing
no definitive sound, no sound in particular.

Pearl

Pale, brittle wings
dissolve in sunlight.
Even the moonshine tail
turns grimy—
the dust of the world
drawn to the in-your-face
display of purity. Rare
as a mistake of divine
proportions, she resists
all attempts at context,
avoids her darker brothers
who sing warnings
about the malignancies
that can spot our souls.

Why should being exposed
make her any better than
the rest? Who says solitude
breeds goodness?
Maybe that's why the hunter
stepped out onto his porch,
raised shotgun to sky
and took aim at the strange
reeling thing.
Maybe he knew how darkness
can thrive on the inside—
understood how easy it is
to hide a blackened heart.

House of Usher

It still surprises you, that the hand
rising from depths of mirror
      never surfaces.
Year after year, you go on
sailing across the lake of happiness,
the light sparking on ordinary fears,
reality a smooth glass
painted with clouds crossing silver.
          How many days
have you traced a fingertip over time
and watched its circles rippling?

True, there are moments when the images—
the child, the house, the dog
sprawled asleep before the fire—waver,
the reflections threatening to dissolve
into a lifetime of bad luck.
And sometimes, late at night,
      when the moon
loses itself behind shadow,
you feel yourself floating along empty hallways.
You know then what you always wanted—
the plunge through darkness, the swimming
toward the lost twin, the one true self.

Wolves

I want what they are—
want to hear with their ears,
to sleep in their dens of sensibility.

I've read that wolves can register a leave-fugue falling
from miles away.

A friend once told me they smell the snow
in people's smiles,
the threat curled in a handshake.

Like us, they'll kill for territory or a hurt mate.
Like us, they've been known
to surround what they need and destroy it.

Wolves aren't gods. They survive as we do,
die as we do,
but reflections don't interest me.

At night I lie awake and imagine how the land that's left
welcomes the wild roving of their existence.
Their fur ripples

as they fan out across silver fields,
seeking an ancient, forgotten freedom.

Walking the Dog in Winter

The tree holds sky between its branches—
a cloud and a blue so intense it reminds me
of summer—as if it's possible for a dying,
lonely thing to open its arms and wrap
warmth inside stillness. Of course
nothing actually works like that. The cloud
shakes itself free from the tree's embrace,
refuses to take part in my wishing
this blustery, scattered moment into metaphor.

A long time ago, life flamed complicated
patterns. There were cities, the rush and crush
of love, late nights in bars and unfamiliar
rooms, lights that blurred by or blared neon,
other lights strung across melodious courtyards.
Always there was the swoosh of days—years—
streaming between high buildings.

At the center of the field, the tree waits
with fanned branches and high, delicate
expectations. I'm sure it won't be long
until night comes with its slow dazzle of stars
to teach me a different kind of blossoming.

Devil's Ivy

The sunroom is an explosion of mottled hearts,
tendrils unfurling all the way to the ceiling
as if I'm the right kind of saint—the kind
who can charm life from death's coiled basket.
I don't know what I've done to deserve it.
My grandmother grew roses so deeply red,
her garden seemed more dream than reality.
Even the yard I memorized as a kid held peonies
heavy enough to illuminate night like strings of moons.
This alchemy is a darker quickening, almost impossible
to kill and fed by anything but light.
If I close my eyes I can actually feel them—
the roots of my failures reaching into blackness,
pulling sustenance from an energy so big it scares me.

Autumn Days

The trees glow like stained glass
as the afternoon warms to translucence.

Distance doesn't weigh much now.
Sunlight falls through the gaps between branches.
Red and yellow leaves scatter across neighbors' lawns.

When I think of the things I haven't done,
I don't know anymore if they're important.

I've already forgotten the contours of faces
memorized long ago, contours etched onto the past,
detailed as fingerprints or maps.

Outside, the leaves lift and turn in the wind,
their colors a choreography of change.

On days like this, it seems as if October won't ever end
and happiness will go on chasing its tail forever.

But I believe in winter's silvery light, in its heavy white coat,
in the darkness of unmarked dates on a calendar
and the way the nights fan out across an endless cold.

Terra Incognita

Afterward, I couldn't unthink it—
the idea that it wasn't wind

but sea that reached out
to tug on the string of the kite

and yank it from February air.
Or maybe something else

equally badass. Time,
for example. Mathematics.

Mythology? Because hadn't
that darting, glittering diamond

written its sentence endlessly
across wintery blackboard sky—

as if its flight were nothing
but another riff on Icarus

or a kid kept after school
in a famous, forgotten movie,

the chalk in his hand a rebuke
for nebulous crimes.

Maybe what I really mean
is happiness has its own

buoyancy. A football arcing
over snow-dusted memories.

Ships tilting toward the edge
of unknown. The mind's sails

filling with air, billowing out
beyond loss, past all the old maps

we carry inside us.

Whalom Park

No one ever really believed in her—
the girl whose hair streamed so legendary
that wind reached out
and coiled those gold locks
around the old rollercoaster tracks.
At five and eight, we'd toss her story
back and forth across bedtime,
egging each other on toward terror.

At thirteen I rode my banana bike
past the dark lake, held my breath
until the lights wrapped me in neon's
embrace. For a buck you could buy a ride
on the Ferris wheel, and as it rose
the town laid itself out for me,
making me forget about loneliness.

No one kissed me, but I could almost feel
the heat of a boy's hands under my halter top,
taste his tongue parting sugared lips.
I still do sometimes, my mind held motionless
at a stoplight where rows of condos
document a world gone dull—
the past rattling inside the present
like a filament in a burned-out bulb.

Radioactive Fountain of Youth

Punta Gorda, Florida

There's something rotten in eternity.
Spigot full of sulfites—hell scent
or maybe just the occasional waft
of boiled eggs settling onto skin.
As for the rest, it's better not to think
about it. Better to lay the suit out across
the bed, polish the shoes, leave
flattering photos in strategic places.

But what of the child down the street,
the one with the sapphire eyes? On TV,
she said she learned to swim in those waters—
told America how she frolicked in a hotel
pool of forever, oblivious to science.
No one understood anything back then,
she said, only knew the mirrors in the lobby
gleamed like starlight, moondust, first love.

Now there's only a rusted warning sign
in an empty lot. And the child: whereabouts
unknown. Now nobody comes except a guy
who attaches a hose to wash his Mustang.
On TV, the car sat under ordinary sky
like any other, but when it sputtered off camera
you could almost see it—tires burning down the strip
and sun shining hot on chrome.
Somewhere beyond oblivion, the radio blares
as a lost girl leans her head out the window,
glossy gold hair still streaming
tails of sparks across neon desert.

Spontaneous Combustion

This is the year I fall for tacky lawn displays,
striped tights, slasher movies no one over thirty
watches. The year the house
slips out of suspended animation,
as if I've finally stopped expecting
my ex's mother to show up and invite herself in.

In the yard, a rake lies out in the rain
and leaves skitter past clear boundaries.
I tell myself I'll pick up where I left off.
I tell myself the recent incident
at the self-serve island was a fluke.
I try to forget the cashier running with cones,
the man who jumped out of his car
and waved both arms at me,
gasoline sloshing around my sneakers.
As if I didn't know the meaning of full anymore.

The truth is, this has to be the year
I buy the red coat, the red boots, the
silly red sweater woven with sparkly yarn.
Save polar bears. Protest somnambulism.
Learn relativity and/or dead languages.
Tear the beating hearts out of men
in sad honky-tonk bars.
Because how much time do any of us,
even the luckiest, have?

The embers in the grate die innocuously.
No mess, no fuss, nothing
that can't be swept up and set out with the trash.
An example of what? A metaphor for what?
The truth is, I don't know the meaning
of full anymore so I sit at home
in my sparkly invisible sweater and stinky shoes.
Imagine you, me, anyone, opening a door
and tossing a match onto dreaming.
See the fumy pictures flare—catch fire.
Feel this bent willow body blaze.

4

Hungry clouds swag on the deep.
—William Blake

The Rain

remembers the water in us,
falls silver

under streetlamps on the other side
of the street.

Somewhere a dog runs through the rain
as a man climbs out of a car door.

His umbrella blooms like a black flower.

On a lit porch his wife waits
for their child to come home.

There are rivers inside us all,
blue branches

flowing toward the heart,

and the rain falls and goes on falling,

streaming across the night, as it carries us back

to the wide, dark sea.

Nightmare

for my daughter

Your voice flickers in silence
like light slanting down
through fathoms of sleep.
In bare feet and a Batman T-shirt,
you fight your way out of emptiness,
stumble toward familiar.

Your mind lags behind,
still dreaming dark places.
The dog raises his head
but whether it's the sound
of fear that rouses him
or the jangle of words
I've tossed at you all at once
I'm not sure.

In the end you settle for a hug
that doesn't really
do much of anything, then
pad back across the hallway
to the cave of aloofness
all teenagers live in.
Come morning we'll resurrect
the argument about angel wing
tattoos and chicken-pox piercings
in unacceptable places.
But for now time's small
as a newborn's grasp.
I can hold the distance between your first and last cry
between the whisper of breathing,
the beat of a pulse.

Shore

Pale, pewter sky, as if the day
were an old painting,
its colors faded past fixing.

Or maybe it was just that the rain
had washed the light too many times.

Either way, the yellow kite
churned in the early spring sea

and I could taste the salt on my lips,
the storm's long shadow,

as my grandfather waded out past safety
to bring back what was mine.

On the beach our coats flapped around our bodies
and someone's hat
skipped across the sand.

We never had a conversation
or went anywhere alone,

and I still wonder what it meant, or if it meant
anything at all—
that plunging into weather

after a string unspooling from my hands
into water's deep forgetting.

Peace Roses

*When the Nazi invasion of France seemed imminent, Francis Meilland
sent eyes of the plant to rose growers that he knew in Turkey, Germany,
Italy, and the United States. —Connie Krochmal*

They've electrified the rain.

The kitchen table's a fallen chandelier,
each bloom its own sun, a yellow halo
       of crimson-
           tipped
              petals
                  flaring.

Nights I hear them humming bees' jazz.

They're in constant dialogue with the refrigerator,
the light over the stove,
an orange chair in the basement.

My mind's a hive
         heavy with syrupy dreams
but the taste of ash burns my tongue.

Always there's the same residue of ghosts
marching to the tune of Hitler's "Taps."

You can break a magnet in half,
but you can't unsnap its poles.

Smokestack against sky.

Dark's moth-eaten blanket thrown over light.

The unbroken silence that sleeps
in every newborn's first cry.

Beautiful Blueberries

last entry in the journal of Chris McCandless

I imagine them round in my hand,
each world offering

a simple kind of sustenance,
a sweetness that holds back,

suggests sky, lake, summer
without making any promises.

It's true that I don't know
exactly what I'm hungry for.

Some days I'm certain it's only
a matter of diligence,

know if I can find the right
word, I'll be able to pour

all my desire into its syllables,
fill sound to the brim.

Some days I think about silence,
how it bells out across the air,

its circles smoothing restless,
rumpled talk the way a mother

in a painting touches the forehead
of a sick child and lets sleep

settle onto life's fevered dream.

After Writing 38 Poems

I want to write about lakes,
their cold spring-fed clarity
and deepening blues, want
to write about rivers running
fast but smooth by me,
to imagine lines flowing
from a place I've never been
or even known, at least not well.
But peace hasn't caught up yet,
the words bees in my mouth,
a thousand suns needling sleep.
Everywhere in the house light slants
through glass, its knives hot on my skin.
Outside the air funnels into silence,
filling its empty wind socks
and crying out *beauty, misery.*

Just Reply Yes Only

      The peonies from the garden
make a vase full of blowsy ghosts.
         Oh, how I want to be that decadent—
to whirl around the kitchen wearing all my spirit petticoats
on the outside. Instead I read an email from Richard
   whose proposal will give us two million
         in seven days.

No one reads email anymore.

      So I sit at the table not reading my email
and watch the squirrels gorge themselves on birdseed.
      The birds aren't anywhere obvious.
They may as well be in Florida. Why not?

Likewise, some days I think you love me,
      imagine us getting it on et cetera
in your '76 Chevy while Gabriel plays on the radio.
   In my imagination,
kissing you is an honest-to-God cherry blossom,
   a bee-stung sex kitten, a till-death-do-us-part
crossword only we can solve.

This isn't one of those days.

So I go back to my fat squirrels and my peonies
standing in for God and to Richard,
     poor, dear Richard,
waiting somewhere in Spambot City for his answer.

Map of a Minor Requiem

It wasn't like being locked
out of a house, standing
simply on the wrong side
of windows—either/or solutions
lounging around in tuxedos.
It wasn't winter with its certainty
of leaves, spring a green glove
worn inside out. This forgetting
a whole new language of loss,
an image glossy with impenetrable
shine, hard on the outside
like a little Fabergé egg.

In the photograph we're
sitting at the edge of a lake.
Fire spreads its hair across the water
as you raise one arm to sky
and give life the finger.
Wait. There is no photograph.
No lake. No light to scallop water.
I'm off-camera, hiding
in a permutation of clouds.
You could be anywhere.
Inscribing *pi* across infinities
of matchbooks. Traveling
light in the company of zombies.
Crashing at last on the edge
of death's magic peacock carpet.

Porcupine

Black glistening of fur
quills gone
it taps its claws
on my cellar window
lolls away the day
sleeps excessively
in pockets of shadow
fallen across
unmown lawn.
And I don't like it
at all, seeing
such a dark thing
exposed.

Later when we go out—
its death sprawled
under sun—
we don't stop.
We've got places to go
where we need to
be. Anyway, I'm not
upset. We all wear
perpetually our armor
until one day we
don't.

At the Edge of Forever

I once heard a story about a boy
who fell into oblivion
off the side of a cliff.
According to my friend,
the boy's falling was a stone
flung into the pond of his faith,
and sometimes that life
hurled so suddenly into emptiness
still ripples across belief's surface.

Now my friend scuba dives,
spends his time deep
beneath layered water.
I'll probably die this way,
he says, *but I don't mind.*
In the ordinary atmosphere,
I see him swimming through darkness,
what's left of his life
undulating past what's unknown.

It's late afternoon. Light
slants through the curtains
and pools on the floor.
The house brims with velvet
chairs and solid tables.
Books, DVDs, old photos,
and off in a corner a pair
of ceramic hands
with matching heart lines.
And, yes, I've enmeshed
life in safety, but don't mistake
my meaning. One day or another
I know I'll meet it anyway—
the moment that reaches out to pull me back
into place among the infinities.

Still Life with Latte

There aren't any birds in this poem
and nothing blue.
     The café is a scattering
of the usual laptops and phones,
     bent heads,
hooded eyes.

Outside, the rain falls in silver sheets
across the parking lot.

I think about walking out
        into all that water
and decide against it,

unsure what rebellion would look like
doused with cold, wet,
       colorless afternoon.
A symbol can only take you so far.

Still, I let myself imagine
the moment I'd leap up
    and turn the uncomfortably
ergonomic chair on its side

in a single motion, see myself
    rush across silence,
arms flailing at technology on my way
      to the free side of glass.

But then the idea closes its curtain
and I shift in the
    uncomfortably ergonomic
chair, my coffee placid
    in its cardboard cup.

No one looks up.

Outside, the rain falls in silver sheets.

Daylight Savings

Woke late out of a dream
about kissing a man
I shouldn't have,

but the clock on the dresser glows
     a superfluous hour,
its neon circle
suspended from morning's low branch
         ready for plucking.

Not sure I want it. For one thing,
in springtime, when the world
     shimmers green,
I'll only have to give it back.

And it's not as if I can let consciousness
slip back into the illicit
    rush of all that kissing.

Better to hoard the unused hours for a decade or so
in case of emergency—

or choose each one a little more carefully,
the way people craft albums
    out of only the photogenic poses
and trash the rest.

Maybe best of all is to release them at once—
leave time for the tail end of light
when every second flickers,
     casting just enough life
to fuel the ticking of the heart,
       the last breath
an explosion of stored moments,
     a blaze of unleashed infinities.

Wailing Wall

Red squares of paper fan out,
the handwritten prayers
on their pale sides exposed.
According to the sign,
a girl will fold them into cranes,
then fly across the ocean
to lay the birds in crevices
between sadness.

They say the wall is a direct line
to God, that wishes rise with dawn
and drift on currents of thought
until they reach the border
between body and spirit, between
this world and the next.

I don't know if I believe in them
or not, these firebirds that ignite hope
and claim to rekindle
what's been lost. I don't know
what lives inside absence.
At the heart of death is darkness,
but what is darkness?
Is it a stone lodged in eternity,
the soul a rough, uncut sun?

I drop my unborn phoenix
into a manila envelope
filled with origami incantations—
the red square still blank,
an absence calling another absence.
If anyone hears,
let them catch silence as it climbs,
cup in a question's hands
blankness as it burns.

Moon Jellies

Even the name sounds silly,
as if they're the kind of creatures

you'd find in Whoville
or maybe at the bottom

of a cereal box. No brains,
no nerves, no bones,

almost nothing but water
and veils that haunt

surfaces of absence—
bodies guileless, lives

rocked by tides
singing old equations.

The ghosts of their shadows
drift over muddy graves

of dinosaurs and saber-
toothed tigers, pterodactyls

and woolly mammoths—
the sum of survival

caught in a translucence of bells,
a net of whole notes

rippling across forever
from cathedrals of light.

Physics

Even kids know the basics nowadays. Planets strapped
into the time-space Tilt-A-Whirl. Schrödinger's cat in its black
not-box, existence flickering like a defective lightbulb.
Dark matter! Dark matter stretching its long-armed infinities,
elbowing out the rest of the universe. Personally, I don't
understand any of it. You tell me we're starfire and dead light,
particle and wave. God is a wizard, you say, waiting behind a half-
closed curtain, hoping no one's dog will dare pull back mystery
and reveal His too-human soul. Which nobody will, you say,
mostly because we're a hell of a lot more concerned about our
own souls, not to mention the souls of mothers, fathers, children,
grandparents, friends, enemies, teachers, infatuations, horses,
dogs, cats, and (occasionally) goldfish. Who can argue with that?
In origami dreams I see my grandfather wading into winter sea,
fishing for a drowned kite. My grandmother's face falling in on
itself, bones laced with pain. The girl with the noose around her
throat kicking the alarm clock off the table. The infant swaddled
in forever. And, yes, you—even you, you smug son of a bitch,
you fading (even now) before me, a little (every day) before me—
you with your singing silences, your badass roses, your any-other-
name antics, shut up (sooner, later) in death's black not-box,
all your particles, your waves gone (gradually, suddenly) still.
Still—if you, I or anybody is both particle and wave, here and
not here, what else is there to do but press our lips to flesh
and taste the sting of all roads winding away from innocence?
Let the boats of our senses rock us toward redemption.
Let the tides of our bodies drift, endlessly, toward love.

Spirit Bear

I want to believe in
this ghost and its snowy
magic. Because I can
feel the arctic deep
inside, I still don't trust
the thaw. Only the bear,
pale as moonlight, reminds
me the world was ice, too,
when Raven spread his wings
and fanned the white
until absence flamed green.
Only the bear with his wind paws
can show me what Earth saw
with newborn eyes,
what she heard in silence.
Pine spires unfurling
to point us toward heaven,
its universal fires. Lakes
beginning to mirror blue.
The first bird lifting sound
in its beak and stringing
from branch to branch
the notes of our survival.

Milkweed

Summer split open.
Heat, blue sky
hollowed out.

The side of the road
is a sea of blackened pods
and dark stalks,

but all around us the air
glimmers handfuls of floss—
seeds floating

on currents invisible,
dissolving in light.
How I want to believe

in this version of loss—
this place where
whatever survives

becomes wind,
weightless, unbound
as an ordinary day

opening its spaces.

Canción de los Huesos

after La Loba, who sings over a wolf skeleton to resurrect it

You'd forgotten about the desert, its streaming night sounds
    and blazing heat. It comes to you now

in a waking dream, reds and oranges layered across sky
    bleeding into sand. Your heaven

burning between Pleistocene clouds, locked inside distance.

You hold out your ghost hands in search of a key,
    turn up your palms and follow the ghost rivers

branching across the place where your pulse beat.

Nothing there. Nothing there.

The shooter's mind a forest of spiders, upside-down bats.

He'll appear for no reason and fire himself again
    into Phoenix-wing fame.

He'll be wearing a new name, a new town.

You won't know him by the slope of his shoulders, the swiftness
    of his gait, though the blood in his voice
    will stumble you into memory.

Close your ghost eyes against it.

You are searching for the bones curved in riverbeds and caves.

You scatter them across the emptiness,
    leave birds and deer behind.

lips fluttering against your collarbone, the baby clapping her hands

Leave them. Leave them.

You are searching for the wolf skeleton
    that gleams in a canyon's copper bowl.

When you find it, you will sit before your death and sing to it.
    Its fur, its dark eyes, its howl.

You will sing to your wolf death and admire its fangs.
   Watch night's throat rip open.

Witness the violent spill of stars.

On the Road

Sometimes the words
step out of the poem
and you can see all the way
to meaning's horizon,
the images transparent
as sky in winter,
the air fading to a color
you can't name.

That's when you notice
the house aglow
at the edge of seeing,
its row of windowpanes
flickering uncertainties
that tempt you
to set out on a journey
that might change your life,
might not.

Salmon Run

You leave the sea behind
to return to the birth river
you fled years before,
the sun firing sky as
peripheral as night's
pinprick constellations.
You've learned how to live
without them. Your only
compass is inside you—
pointing always
toward the unseen star,
the upstream mind—
which is why it surprises
you to find your swimming
is really a circle,
a completion of time
that the ones before you
wound before you were born.
Listen. Their ghost hearts
beat drums in your veins
and everyone you ever loved
courses through you.
Listen. Your blood leaps waterfalls
as you rise into the dark
surge of endless beginning.

Acknowledgments

I am grateful to the editors of the following publications in which these poems previously appeared. I would also like to thank the Origami Poems Project for nominating "The Blue Earrings" for a 2017 Pushcart Prize. Last but never least, I want to thank my daughter Caitlyn, my family, Benjamin Grajales and Anuj Patel for their help and support.

Binnacle: "Morning After"
Bitter Oleander: "Van Gogh"
BlazeVOX: "The Explorer's Dream," "Reading," "To the Guy Who Posted About Kittens on His Doorstep"
Borderlands: Texas Poetry Review: "Red Mendelssohn," "Sanibel Island"
failbetter: "Wintering"
Kentucky Review: "Bottle Tree, 1831," "Little Risks," "X-Ray"
Hayden's Ferry Review: "Canción de los Huesos"
The Journal: "The House"
The Lindenwood Review: "The Rain"
The Literary Review: "Rothko No. 8, 1952"
The Meadow: "Black Sheep Café"
Meat for Tea: "Devil's Ivy," "The Snow Is Always Greener"
The Mom Egg: "The Agoraphobic's Dream," "House of Usher," "On the Road"
Mud Season Review: "Dragon," "Conservatory"
New Madrid: "Dinosaur Tracks," "Forecast," "Glass Town"
Phantom Kangaroo: "Ghost Hunters"
Red Paint Hill Journal: "Beautiful Blueberries"
Still: The Journal: "At the Kitchen Window," "Bottle Tree, 1922," "Milkweed," "Still Life"
Storm Cellar: "Mind Fishing"
Switched-on Gutenberg: "Kirlian Effect"
Valparaiso Poetry Review: "Tracks"
Willow Review: "Interior"

"Coming Attractions" first appeared in the chapbook *Diary in Irregular Ink* (ELJ Editions, 2014).

"Jellyfish," "Birch Forest, 1903" and "The Blue Earrings" appeared in the micro-chapbook *Endless After All* (Origami Poems Project, 2016).

"Scary Story" appeared in the anthology *The Doll Collection* (Terrapin Books, 2016).

About FutureCycle Press

FutureCycle Press is dedicated to publishing lasting English-language poetry books, chapbooks, and anthologies in both print-on-demand and Kindle ebook formats. Founded in 2007 by long-time independent editor/publishers and partners Diane Kistner and Robert S. King, the press incorporated as a nonprofit in 2012. A number of our editors are distinguished poets and writers in their own right, and we have been actively involved in the small press movement going back to the early seventies.

The FutureCycle Poetry Book Prize and honorarium is awarded annually for the best full-length volume of poetry we publish in a calendar year. Introduced in 2013, our Good Works projects are anthologies devoted to issues of universal significance, with all proceeds donated to a related worthy cause. Our Selected Poems series highlights contemporary poets with a substantial body of work to their credit; with this series we strive to resurrect work that has had limited distribution and is now out of print.

We are dedicated to giving all of the authors we publish the care their work deserves, making our catalog of titles the most diverse and distinguished it can be, and paying forward any earnings to fund more great books.

We've learned a few things about independent publishing over the years. We've also evolved a unique, resilient publishing model that allows us to focus mainly on vetting and preserving for posterity poetry collections of exceptional quality without becoming overwhelmed with bookkeeping and mailing, fundraising activities, or taxing editorial and production "bubbles." To find out more about what we are doing, come see us at www.futurecycle.org.

The FutureCycle Poetry Book Prize

All full-length volumes of poetry published by FutureCycle Press in a given calendar year are considered for the annual FutureCycle Poetry Book Prize. This allows us to consider each submission on its own merits, outside of the context of a contest. Too, the judges see the finished book, which will have benefitted from the beautiful book design and strong editorial gloss we are famous for.

The book ranked the best in judging is announced as the prize-winner in the subsequent year. There is no fixed monetary award; instead, the winning poet receives an honorarium of 20% of the total net royalties from all poetry books and chapbooks the press sold online in the year the winning book was published. The winner is also accorded the honor of being on the panel of judges for the next year's competition; all judges receive copies of all contending books to keep for their personal library.

www.ingramcontent.com/pod-product-compliance
Lightning Source LLC
Chambersburg PA
CBHW072359090426
42741CB00012B/3080